DATE DUE

What's So Super About

the

SUPERNATURAL?

Robert Gardner

Twenty-First Century Books
Brookfield, Connecticut

Cover photograph courtesy of © The Stock Market/Dale O'Dell, 1987

Photographs courtesy of UPI/Corbis-Bettman: pp. 24, 34, 59; Hulton Getty/Liaison Agency: p. 28; Photo Researchers, Inc.: p. 41 (David Parker/Science Photo Library)
Illustrations by Network Graphics
Designed by Carole Desnoes

Library of Congress Cataloging-in-Publication Data

Gardner, Robert, 1929–
What's so super about the supernatural? / by Robert Gardner.
p. cm
Includes bibliographical references and index.
Summary: Discusses ESP, psychokinesis, ghosts and apparitions, UFOs and extraterrestrials and other paranormal phenomena, as well as some of the hoaxes that have been perpetrated involving the supernatural.
ISBN 0-7613-3228-6 (lib. bdg.)
1. Parapsychology—Juvenile literature. 2. Supernatural—Juvenile literature.
[1. Parapsychology. 2. Supernatural.] I. Title.
BF1031.G15 1998
133—dc21   98-27062
                                                                         CIP AC

Published by Twenty-First Century Books
A Division of The Millbrook Press, Inc.
2 Old New Milford Rd.
Brookfield, Connecticut 06804

Contents

Introduction

If you read, watch television, and go to the movies, you know that many people are interested in supernatural things and events. There is an abundance of stories, reports, and programs about ESP (extrasensory perception), UFOs (unidentified flying objects), aliens, astrology (the influence of heavenly bodies on human lives), ghosts, channeling (spirit communication), and other paranormal phenomena—events that cannot be explained by scientific laws or theories. Aliens and vampires are popular subjects for movies (the best was probably *E.T. The Extra-Terrestrial*); the sale of good-luck charms is a booming business; most newspapers include daily horoscopes; and even the Internet offers psychic hot-line networks.

At the time this is being written, *The X-Files* is a popular television program among adults and teenagers, and *Sabrina the Teenage Witch*—which features a talking cat and a "spell" a minute—is a favorite of many young viewers. Stephen King is a bestselling author whose frightening stories often involve supernatural happenings. However, authors and TV producers don't always agree on what supernatural material will attract an audience. *X-Files* producer, Chris Carter, rejected one script that Stephen King had prepared for the show, but used another script by the author.

Not everyone succumbs to infatuation with the paranormal. In a Danbury, Connecticut, newspaper, *The News-Times*, a rational reader's letter to the editor requested that the horoscope section contain a preface indicating that the material is for entertainment and should not be taken seriously. The same writer pointed out that most of the predictions about the future made by psychics have not come true and that most significant events that did occur had not been predicted by the same psychics.

A study by Glenn Sparks at Purdue University, in Indiana, has shown that the more people read, watch, or hear about the paranormal, the more likely they are to believe in supernatural powers. That many people watch and/or read about the supernatural is borne out by a recent poll by *Newsweek* magazine. The poll revealed that nearly half of all Americans believe UFOs are real; nearly one-third think aliens—beings from another world—have made contact with us earthlings; and 48 percent believe the government is covering up the truth about UFOs and aliens. In a 1994 Gallup poll of 1,016 adults, 19 percent believed it likely that flying saucers exist, 31 percent thought their existence to be somewhat likely, 43 percent doubted their reality, and about 7 percent were not sure. In that same poll, nearly one fourth of those surveyed believed in astrology, and more than one fourth believed in both reincarnation and our ability to communicate with the dead.

Of all the UFOs investigated by the United States Air Force, only about 2 percent turn out to be truly unidentifiable. The rest are found to be astronomical objects such as stars and planets, various types of aircraft, satellites, weather balloons, or hoaxes. A twenty-one-year study ended in 1969 with a committee concluding that there was no evidence that UFOs were extraterrestrial. Believers argue, of course, that the report was part of a government cover-up designed to keep the truth from the public.

Parapsychology is the study of activities that extend beyond those related to our usual five senses—sight, hearing, smell, touch, and taste. Psychics are people who claim to have a "sixth sense." Whether or not they are truly psychic is open to question. In this book you will have an opportunity to make up your own mind about the validity of parapsychology, which is usually divided into ESP and psychokinesis (PK).

ESP is an ability to receive or transmit information without using the five senses. It consists of telepathy and clairvoyance. Telepathy, sometimes called mind reading, is the transfer of thoughts or information from one mind to another. Clairvoyance—also called remote viewing—is the awareness of an object, a person, or a happening that is beyond the range of the usual senses. It may involve precognition (knowledge of future events) or retrocognition (knowledge of past events).

PK, often called "mind over matter," is the ability to affect material objects without touching them. For example, some people claim they can bend spoons or other objects or make bodies levitate (float in air) without actually touching or lifting them.

It is possible to conduct experiments to test for ESP and PK. In Chapter 4 you will find a series of experiments that will allow you to collect data to determine whether or not you or others have ESP or PK. In the same chapter you will learn how to conduct a séance (a meeting for the purpose of receiving spirit communications), test for the reliability of the Ouija board, bring a spirit's "touch" to a friend, and make your own snow version of crop circles. Other aspects of the paranormal are less open to scientific study. Such things as ghosts, psychic surgery, channeling, alien abductions, flying saucers, fairies, and other supernatural phenomena can be investigated through careful observation and analysis, but it is difficult to design experiments to test for their existence.

Many magicians and mind readers tell their audiences that what they do involves trickery. They admit that they have no paranormal powers and condemn and often expose those who claim to have such ability. People still enjoy watching telepathic and magic feats even when they know the performers lack any psychic capacity.

In Chapter 5 you will have an opportunity to perform a number of stage tricks that might convince viewers that you possess ESP, PK, and other psychic powers such as an ability to read minds and see with your fingers. You can have lots of fun conducting such performances. At the same time you will see how easy it is for you or anyone else to appear to have supernatural ability.

Concrete evidence, such as a spaceship or aliens, has never been available for scientists to examine. In fact, there is no firm scientific evidence for the existence of any supernatural phenomena. Nevertheless, the statistics given in this introduction indicate that people want to believe in individuals of this world—or another—who have powers that cannot be explained. They want to believe the impossible is possible. This belief can be illustrated by an experience shared by illusionist Milbourne Christopher in his book, *Mediums, Mystics, and the Occult*.

In 1957 Christopher visited Cuba a few days before the drawing of the winning number for the $100,000 national lottery. He carried with him a sealed envelope in which, he told the media, were the winning digits for the lottery. Christopher, who was careful to point out that he was a magician and not a psychic, gave the envelope to the Cuban Chamber of Commerce, and it was placed in a guarded safe. Despite his carefully worded statement, he was swamped with calls from people who wanted to know the winning numbers. In fact, the government, fearing he might be kidnapped, provided him with bodyguards to protect him until after the drawing. Of course, he did not really know the winning number and, therefore, could not have revealed it had he been carried off by those who so firmly believed he was psychic.

After the drawing for the lottery, the guarded envelope was opened. Sure enough, the winning number (20050) was found inside. Christopher never revealed how he did it, and, despite his constant reminders that he was a magician and not a psychic, many Cubans were convinced he was clairvoyant. They, like many other people who are told that the seemingly impossible is the result of trickery and not paranormal powers, still want to believe in the supernatural rather than accept the fact that they were tricked by a clever magician, medium, or fortune-teller.

In his book *The Demon-Haunted World*, astronomer Carl Sagan wrote: " . . . we humans have a talent for deceiving ourselves. Skepticism must be a component of the explorer's tool kit, or we will lose our way. There are wonders enough out there without our inventing any."

CHAPTER one

ESP, PK, and Other Paranormal Phenomena

Many examples of ESP have been described in newspapers and magazines or on radio and television. President Abraham Lincoln was said to have had a clairvoyant sense of his assassination. And the prediction of John F. Kennedy's assassination made clairvoyant Jeane Dixon famous. On the other hand, if you were constantly surrounded by bodyguards as every president is, it would be difficult not to have premonitions of being assassinated.

One strange account of telepathy is the tale of an American farmer named James Chaffin who placed his last will in his father's Bible. According to the story, he never told anyone about the will or where he had placed it. After he died an earlier will was found and opened. In it he left his entire estate to his third son. His wife and three other sons received nothing. Several years later his second son had a vivid dream in which his father appeared wearing a black overcoat. In the dream his father said, "Look in the pocket of my overcoat."

When the overcoat was found, there was a note in the pocket: "Read the 27th chapter of Genesis in my father's Bible." In that Bible they found a will stating that his estate was to be divided equally among all his sons and his wife. Despite protests from the third son, the court ruled that the latest document found in the Bible represented the dead man's true will.

Was this an example of telepathy between the dead man and his son? Was it a son's clairvoyance? Or did the second son suddenly remember something his father had told him long ago, something he had forgotten until the ruminations of his unconscious mind caused it to surface in a dream?

ESP Research

The problem with telepathy, clairvoyance, and most instances of parapsychology is that it is usually impossible to tell whether we are witnessing a truly paranormal phenomenon or an event with a natural explanation. Nevertheless, parapsychologists do conduct experiments to try to provide evidence for the existence of ESP.

Pioneer research in ESP was begun by Dr. Joseph Rhine at Duke University, in North Carolina, during the 1930s. He used what are called Zener cards to test people for ESP. A deck of Zener cards consists of twenty-five cards with five each of five different designs. Figure 1–1 shows the different designs that usually appear on the cards.

In Rhine's experiment, a person in one room (a sender) would remove the top card from a shuffled deck of Zener cards and concentrate on the card for exactly one minute in an effort to send a "signal" by telepathy. At the same time, a subject in another room (a receiver) with a clock set to the same as the sender's would try to pick up the signal and record which of the symbols (shown in Figure 1) he or she thought the sender was trying to transmit by telepathy. Because the receiver had a choice of only five different symbols, he or she would choose the right one 20 percent (1/5) of the time just by guessing. Consequently, Rhine

FIGURE 1 These are Zener cards. They are used to test people for ESP.

looked for those people who, over many trials, consistently had a success rate greater than 20 percent. He found that the chances of a person scoring better than 20 percent in "receiving" the correct signal improved if both sender and receiver were relaxed, in a quiet environment, and believed ESP to be possible.

In one trial a receiver scored 119 hits (correct choices) out of 300 cards. Even doubters agreed that this score of nearly 40 percent, twice that expected by chance alone, was phenomenal. The probability of obtaining such results by chance is astronomically small—about 1 in 100 billion trillion (10^{23}). Such results certainly indicated the existence of ESP, at least for this particular pair of experimenters.

After visiting the site at Duke University where the experiment had been conducted, scientist C. E. H. Hansel showed that the person receiving the signals could have cheated. There were windows opening into the room occupied by the sender. The person receiving the signals could have seen the cards being viewed by the sender. By standing on a chair and peeking into the room, Hansel was able to correctly choose the symbol on twenty-two of twenty-five cards turned over in the same way as they were in the original experiment. Furthermore, although Rhine was able to find a number of people who seemed to have ESP, other experimenters were unable to obtain similar results when they repeated his experiment many times.

Scientific truth, as revealed by experiment, should hold true for all experimenters. Since other scientists could not duplicate Rhine's results, his work remained suspect. Most scientists believe that ESP does not exist.

You can make up your own mind about ESP by doing Activities 1–4 in Chapter 4.

Animal ESP

Some people believe animals have either ESP or senses so much keener than ours that they can detect signals we cannot. For example, one man found that when his dog began barking at him, he should seek a safe place because within ten minutes he would have an epileptic seizure and lose consciousness. Somehow the dog appeared to be able to sense that something was wrong. Does an epileptic emit an odor that dogs can detect, or do they have ESP?

Other people claim their pets can anticipate their arrival. The animals are somehow aware that their owner's presence is imminent and will watch from a window or wait by a door. Of course, some such behavior is time oriented. A dog expects a child to return from school or an adult from work at about the same time each day. But some pets show similar behavior even when family members arrive at odd or unexpected times.

Some people believe that dogs and other animals can anticipate an earthquake. Snakes, mice, and other animals that live underground are said to leave their burrows. Bottom-dwelling fish move to the surface. Ants move their eggs. Dogs, horses, and pheasants become noisy and exhibit nervous behavior. Do these animals hear or feel the small vibrations that precede an earthquake, or do they have a sixth sense (ESP)? Whether such signs are a valid means of predicting earthquakes is questioned by many seismologists (people who study earthquakes).

To carry out an experiment to see if your own pet has ESP, try Activity 5 in Chapter 4.

Psychokinesis

As you know, psychokinesis (PK), or mind over matter, is the ability to influence objects without any direct physical contact. One of the best-known people to seem to exhibit PK powers is Uri Geller, an Israeli. Geller was brought to the United States by Andrija Puharich, who claimed to have come from the distant planet Hoova and traveled to Earth on board the spaceship *Spectra*. It was from Hoova that Geller supposedly received the invisible force that enabled him to bend spoons and other metal objects by simply staring at them or gently rubbing them. The same force enabled him to move watch hands, drive cars while blindfolded, read minds, and move compass needles.

Uri Geller's demonstrations of spoon bending and other psychokinetic phenomena convinced many of his PK powers, but not everyone. When Geller appeared on the television program *60 Minutes* during the 1970s, TV producer James Jackson asked magician Milbourne Christopher how to make sure that Geller could not resort to trickery. Christopher told him not to let Geller touch anything that would later be used on the show and to have someone watch his hands at all times. As a result, Geller was not able to bend metal or start broken watches while on camera with Mike Wallace. James "The Amazing" Randi, a talented magician, gave similar advice before Geller appeared on Johnny Carson's late-night show. Geller's PK powers were nowhere to be seen that night as well. They appeared, however, when he was a guest on Merv Griffin's show, where no attempt was made to prevent trickery.

As magicians, both Christopher and Randi know that Geller and others distract the audience while quickly bending a spoon or a key or substituting a slightly bent one for the original. Another trick is using a nail that is slightly bent in the middle. When the slight bend is turned away from the audience, they see what appears to be a straight nail. As the magician rubs the nail, he turns it slightly so that the bend becomes visible to the audience.

For a hands-on, experimental look at PK, turn to Activities 6–8 in Chapter 4.

Psychic Surgery

Psychic surgeons, who seem to be most common in South America and Southeast Asia, claim that they can perform operations with their bare hands. Patients with terminal cancer are often conned into letting a psychic surgeon "operate." What these psychic surgeons actually do is to squeeze some flesh with one hand, while they pretend to make an incision with a finger of the other hand. They then hold the flesh with one hand, while the bent fingers of the other hand appear to be under the patient's skin reaching for the diseased organs or tissue. A false thumb—a thimblelike structure—is used to hold some blood, which is released during the procedure to make it appear as though blood vessels have been severed. An assistant hands the surgeon a cotton-covered balloon filled with a lump of fatty animal tissue or the internal parts of a chicken. The surgeon breaks the balloon and pretends to pull tissue or organs from the patient's body. He then draws the skin together, which is "miraculously" rejoined without the need for stitches and is left without a scar. And why should there be? The skin was never cut.

Recently, some of these so-called surgeons have actually cut the patient's flesh in an effort to make the operation more realistic. Since the scalpels are usually not sterilized, infections often follow the procedure.

Because psychic surgeons are not licensed, most of them do not accept money for their services. However, their patients are charged excessive fees for travel, food, and hotel accommodations. They are also encouraged to make sizable donations.

Randi's Challenge

James Randi has offered $10,000 to any person who can demonstrate proof of a truly supernatural phenomenon such as PK, ESP, psychic surgery, ghosts, and channeling (see Chapter 2 for the last two of these).

As you might guess, no psychic surgeon has ever met Randi's challenge. In fact, although many have tried, no one has managed to demonstrate any truly supernatural phenomenon. Randi's money and offer remains; he is not too worried about risking so much money.

One woman who sought to win Randi's $10,000 offer claimed she could see without her eyes. While blindfolded, she read the *New York Times*. Randi noticed that she held the newspaper to her left as she read. When he placed an additional cover over her right eye, she could no longer read the print and began inventing words. A careful look at the goggles she used as a blindfold revealed a small crack on the left side of the right goggle. Because the woman had an unusually concave nose, she could see over her nose with her right eye. Thus, by holding the paper to her left, she could see the print through the crack in the right goggle.

A number of people have claimed to "feel" colors, read by touching print, and see through opaque objects. Careful tests show that they peek. Almost any blindfold will allow a person to peek. A facial grimace leaves a space between the blindfold and the face that enables enough light to reach the eyes so that the person can see. Another trick is to make pinholes through the center of the blindfold. Such holes allow the blindfolded person to see quite well if he or she looks straight ahead in bright light.

Thought Photographs

People have claimed they can take photographs of the images in their minds. A camera is turned toward the photographer's head, a small tube hidden in the photographer's hand is held in front of the camera's lens, and the shutter is opened for a short time. Sometimes when the film is developed, an image of a building or a scene appears on the finished print. Are these really photographs of a mental image, or is trickery involved?

In the 1960s, in response to the claims of Ted Serios, one such mind photographer, James Randi picked up a small tube and held it against a TV camera. The images seen on the monitor closely resembled those seen in thought photographs. Randi suggested that mind photography was a trick, and the secret was in the tiny tube held against the camera's lens.

You can check up on Randi's analysis of mind photography by doing Activity 9 in Chapter 4.

Dowsing

Dowsers claim they have an ability to locate water for well drilling and metal for mining; some even claim they can detect illness by dowsing. A dowser who searches for water beneath the ground is sometimes called a water witch. References to dowsing for water go back to ancient Egypt and Rome. The process usually involves a forked stick—a divining rod—that the dowser carries, one fork in each hand (see Figure 2) as he or she

FIGURE 2 Dowsers claim they can locate underground water with a forked stick. The stick turns when it is above water.

walks along the ground. According to dowsers, the single end of the stick turns down when it is over water. Some even say they can predict the depth that water will be found and the rate at which it flows. Dowsers searching for metal often use metal hangers as divining rods.

Henry Gross was a dowser made famous by Kenneth Roberts, who wrote a book in the mid-twentieth century about him entitled *Henry Gross and His Dowsing Rod*. Roberts claimed that Gross could not only locate water with a forked stick but could do so by talking to the rod as he moved it over a map. Roberts claimed that Gross had found water on Bermuda in just this manner. Only a slight change in position was necessary when Gross went to the island and dowsed with his divining rod. According to Roberts, well drillers did establish freshwater wells at the sites Gross identified despite the fact that water is so scarce in Bermuda that most people there collect rainwater and store it in cisterns.

One critic, T. M. Riddick, called Roberts's book nonsense. He pointed out that dowsers probably have a "land sense" that enables them to find water. As surely as any dowsing rod, low or moist land, soggy land, land that is grassy during a drought, all indicate an aquifer—a water-bearing layer of the earth—close to the surface. Riddick went on to criticize Roberts for his lack of geological knowledge.

No one questions the fact that a divining rod does turn. Dowsers believe they have a special sense, but those who have studied the divining process say the rod turns because of the contraction of involuntary muscles. These are similar, on a larger scale, to the smaller ones involved in the PK experiment found in Activity 7 in Chapter 4. That muscle activity is indeed involved follows from a conversation I had with a dowser. She told me that she knew a fellow dowser for whom the divining rod always turned up rather than down when he was over water. Such a response demonstrates that the rod is not turning because it is attracted to water.

Some studies indicate that dowsers are more sensitive to electromagnetic waves than nondowsers, but what that has to do with dowsing is unclear. Most geologists say that dowsing is hokum. Underground water does not flow in veins but rather saturates the soil beneath a certain level, creating an aquifer. The upper surface of the aquifer is called the water table or water level. Drillers are bound to strike water when they reach the aquifer. In many regions, they could drill anywhere and find water.

When tested by Randi, dowsers always failed to demonstrate their powers. Despite their claims that they would be able to locate water in pipes buried beneath the ground, their success rate was no greater than would be expected by chance. Their divining rods invariably turned, however, if they knew they were standing over water. Randi found that the divining rods of dowsers claiming to be able to detect metal turned when they were held over coins covered with paper. When he placed coins in only one of ten envelopes and spread them over the floor, none of the dowsers could identify the envelope that contained the coins. They blamed their lack of success on metal pipes beneath the floor; however, they fared no better when the test was conducted on a pipe-free surface.

Predicting the Future:
Fortune-Tellers and Psychics

Predicting the future of an individual or a nation is a gift claimed by many but tested by few. Fortune-telling has a long history. Those who claimed to find the future in the stars were and are astrologers. While they seldom have succeeded in predicting the future, astrologers did accumulate a lot of valuable information about the stars and planets: information that led to the science of astronomy. Other fortune-tellers claim they can predict the future by reading tea leaves, the lines in a person's palm, the bumps on their heads, or by gazing into a crystal ball. Still others find the future in playing cards or in a deck of symbolic cards called the tarot, by opening books, or by examining the pattern made by throwing pebbles.

Professional psychics often write newspaper columns and make predictions about what will happen in the coming year, decade, or century. They usually don't tell us how they make their forecasts. Professionals who are experts in a particular area of study also make predictions based on what they foresee as the outcome of work and research going on in their field. Generally, predictions are forgotten unless they turn out to be true, in which case the forecaster reminds us that he or she correctly predicted the future. What these people often fail to tell us is that the other 99 percent of their predictions did not come true.

In 1981 the author Irving Wallace, with his children as co-authors, published *The Book of Predictions*. The predictions in the book were obtained from seven professional psychics—Bertie Catchings, Dennis Conkin, Ann Fisher, Beverly Jaegers, Andrew Reiss, Francie Streiger, and Alan Vaughn. The Wallaces also consulted people such as chemist Willard Libby and anthropologist Ashley Montagu, who were experts in their fields.

The results of the predictions were checked for accuracy fifteen years later by Alan M. Tuerkheimer and Stuart A. Vyse, who reported their findings in the March/April 1997 issue of the *Skeptical Inquirer* in an article entitled "The Book of Predictions Fifteen Years Later." For purposes of comparison, Tuerkheimer and Vyse included predictions from seven experts. Libby and Montagu were joined by science writer Isaac Asimov; David Snyder, an editor of *The Futurist* magazine; computer scientist Eldon Byrd; scientist Edmund Berkeley; and Catholic priest and sociologist Andrew Greeley.

The experts made fewer predictions and limited their forecasts to their field of knowledge. The psychics, on the other hand, made predictions about things that would happen in science, politics, metallurgy, satellites, and many other areas.

The results of their analysis are shown in Table 1. In evaluating the predictions, those that were clear-cut were scored as a "hit" if correct or a "miss" if incorrect. Predictions that were more vague or contained more than one part were scored as a "partial hit " if they were partially correct.

Table 1: Accuracy of predictions made by psychics and experts for the years 1981–1996.*

Psychic	No. of Predictions	Hits	Hits + partial hits	Percentage of hits + partial hits
Bertie Catchings	20	2	3	15
Dennis Conkin	13	3	3	23
Ann Fisher	4	0	1	25
Beverly Jaegers	17	0	3	18
Andrew Reiss	7	0	2	29
Francie Streiger	20	0	0	0
Alan Vaughn	12	1	1	8
	93	6	13	14

Expert	No. of Predictions	Hits	Hits + partial hits	Percentage of hits + partial hits
Isaac Asimov	3	0	0	0
Edmund Berkeley	8	0	2	25
Eldon Byrd	6	1	3	50
Andrew Greeley	6	1	3	50
Willard Libby	8	0	2	25
Ashley Montagu	5	2	3	60
David Snyder	15	4	6	40
	51	8	18	35

* Results taken from "The Book of Predictions Fifteen Years Later" by Alan M. Tuerkheimer and Stuart A. Vyse. *Skeptical Inquirer,* March/April 1997, pp. 40–42.

On the basis of the data in Table 1, what do you conclude about the ability of psychics and experts to predict the future?

CHAPTER two

Ghosts, Spirits, and Mediums

With wolves howling from afar, owls hooting in the trees above, and leaves rustling as field mice run through them, people seated around a campfire enjoy telling and listening to ghost stories that make shivers run up and down their spines and hair rise on the backs of their necks. Most of these frightening stories are fictional, but some are said to be true. One such story is found in C. E. H. Hansel's book *ESP, A Scientific Evaluation*.

Sir Edmund Hornby was chief judge of the Supreme Consular Court of China and Japan, in Shanghai in 1875. According to the story told by Hornby, he had written a judgment and given it to his butler to deliver to reporters the next day. He had then retired at midnight and was soon fast asleep, only to be awakened by a knock on his bedroom door. The judge noted that the time was 1:20 A.M. At the door he found a reporter who looked pale and seemed to be in pain. The reporter wanted a summary of the judgment that Hornby had given to his butler. Although annoyed by the intrusion, the judge, fearing an argument might awaken his wife, gave the reporter a brief recap of his judgment before returning to bed at 1:30.

As the story goes, the next morning Hornby told his wife and butler the story of the intruding reporter. Neither could understand how this could have happened because the doors had been locked earlier in the evening and they were still locked the following morning.

Upon reaching court that morning, the judge was informed that the reporter who had visited him much earlier that same day had been found dead. The reporter's wife said she had left him in his room at approximately midnight. When she returned an hour and a half later, he was dead. A doctor who responded to her call arrived about 2:00 A.M. and said the reporter had been dead about an hour. In his notebook the reporter had written a partially legible account of the judge's decision. The judge ordered an inquest, which revealed that the reporter had died of a heart attack and could not have left his home undetected between 11:00 P.M. and 1:00 A.M. that night.

It was nine years before Judge Hornby told his story to a magazine. He claimed, however, that his memory was very clear and that he was certain he had seen the reporter between 1:20 and 1:30 A.M. on the day the reporter died.

In a later publication of the same magazine, a letter sent to the editors maintained that there were serious discrepancies in the judge's story. The writer of the letter said that the reporter had died not at 1:00 A.M. but at about 8:00 A.M. Furthermore, the judge's wife could not have been present because she had died two years earlier and the judge did not remarry until three months after the event supposedly took place (January 20). Finally, the records show that no judgment was rendered on that day and an inquest never took place.

You might like to investigate a ghost story that you have heard from someone who claims it is true. What do you find?

More Ghosts

This story is one of many ghostly accounts. But most of these stories, if checked, have the same flaws as the one told by the judge. When examined objectively, the facts do not agree with the story as told. Times are wrong, people supposedly seen were known to be elsewhere, descriptions of places do not agree with the same places when seen by others, and so on. Of course, there is no way that such single events can be investigated scientifically.

Haunted houses, however, can be investigated. Frequent observations about a house suspected to be haunted are noises or a light that seems, from outside, to move from room to room. The moving light is often found to be the reflection of car headlights. As the car moves, its lights are reflected off the window in one room, then another and another. Noises are often the result of wind moving through openings in the attic. In one such house, children had placed a toy whistle in an attic knothole. When the wind was coming from the right direction to blow through the whistle, it produced a wailing sound. In another case, the wind sometimes caused a rocking chair to rock on the attic floor. Temperature changes cause timbers to lengthen or shorten, producing creaking sounds as they rub on other boards or timbers. You may hear such sounds in your own home when hot water flowing through pipes and metallic heating units causes them to expand and cooling down makes them contract.

A home in Yorkshire, England, was believed to be haunted because it periodically produced eerie sounds. A careful investigation of the building revealed cracked walls, twisted door frames, and a sagging roof, suggesting that the house was on a shifting foundation. But what could cause a foundation to move?

Further study showed that an old unused sewer ran next to the building. At high tide, water entered the sewer and seeped into the soil under the foundation, causing the building to shift. The periodic nature of the sounds was found to coincide with the tides.

The "Amityville Horror," the Long Island, New York, home of the DeFeo family, was the site of murders that, contrary to the series of movies it spawned, had nothing supernatural about it.

The eerie flickering "ghosts" seen around graveyards or over swampy ground are usually will-o'-the-wisps: burning methane gas. The gas is produced by decaying organic matter and ignited by spontaneous combustion.

Poltergeists

Poltergeists, from the German words *polter* and *geist* meaning "racketing ghost," are noisy ghosts. Reports of poltergeists throwing lamps, books, and other objects usually come from houses where an adolescent lives. One such poltergeist was reported to have invaded a house in Columbus, Ohio, in 1984. An adolescent girl, Tina Resch, lived there. Tina was an adopted child who wanted to know the identity of her biological parents. Newspaper reporters from the *Columbus Dispatch* brought a video camera to her house to photograph and record phones that had been thrown, lamps and ashtrays that had fallen, and noises that were heard.

No ghost was ever seen or heard on camera; however, when the camera was inadvertently left running, the tape showed Tina surreptitiously pulling over a lamp.

A possibly unsolved case is that of a poltergeist who reportedly invaded a home in Cambridge, England, where eleven-year-old Matthew Manning lived. As the disturbances became more violent, Matthew's father went to the police. The police asked Dr. Owen from the Cambridge Psychical Research Society to investigate. Owen found that all poltergeist action ceased when Matthew was away.

On one occasion, Matthew's bed was thrown about and left leaning at an angle against the wall. The next morning the dining room was a wreck, and several knives were missing. Soon after, the family began to find puddles of water on various floors each morning, and warnings reading "Matthew Beware!" were scrawled on walls.

When Matthew left for boarding school, he claimed the poltergeist followed him. As Matthew began to write extensively and produce detailed and delicate drawings in school, the poltergeist activities ceased. Had Matthew found a way to rechannel the poltergeist's energy?

Scientists argue that there is no scientific evidence supporting the existence of ghosts, whether poltergeists or others. In instances where scientists and magicians have investigated poltergeist activity, they have usually found it to be related to a clandestine adolescent or to undiscovered causes that disappeared when they entered the picture.

In 1997 a *Dateline NBC* program broadcast a report about an electronic poltergeist who called himself Sommy. Sommy was using "high-tech" methods to harass the Tamai family in Emeryville, Ontario, Canada. Calls were suddenly disconnected, and strange noises were heard on the line during conversations. The situation worsened when Debbie and Dwayne Tamai went on vacation and left Billy, their fifteen-year-old son, with their housesitting friend, Cheryl McCaulis. The electricity kept going on and off, the PIN (personal identification number) used to access voice mail was changed, and Sommy began making obscene and threatening calls as well as grunts, burps, and other sounds that interrupted phone conversations.

When Debbie and Dwayne returned, they found Cheryl's report unbelievable—until Debbie was herself frightened when Sommy's mean and threatening voice interrupted one of her calls. Soon Sommy was changing TV channels and calling the family with detailed information that he could have known only if he had bugged the house.

The police, the utility company, and private investigators could offer no explanations for Sommy. The Tamais thought that Sommy had installed listening and other electronic devices in the house during its construction but when walls were torn open, none could be found. *Dateline* even hired a security company to investigate the home, but they came up empty after a six-hour-long search.

As the parents prepared to take Billy to the police station to defend him against rumors that accused him of the Sommy-initiated pranks, the enigma was suddenly solved. Billy confessed that he and some friends were behind the electronic poltergeist. The family apologized to those from whom they had sought help and said they were seeking professional counseling for Billy.

Channeling and Spirit Mediums

Channeling, or mediumship, involves using a living body to hold the spirit of someone who is deceased. That spirit then speaks by using the channeler's voice. A woman named J. Z. Knight claims to be in contact with the spirit of a 35,000-year-old person named Ramtha. Ramtha communicates through Knight's voice. Interestingly, he speaks English with what Carl Sagan interpreted as an Indian accent. Of course, Sagan wondered why Ramtha and other spirits who speak through channelers, if they are authentic, don't tell us something of substance. Instead of making bland statements, why doesn't Ramtha tell us why he speaks English, a language that didn't exist 35,000 years ago, or what life was like so long ago?

Mediums sometimes communicate with the dead in a dark room while seated with a group of people around a table. Such a gathering in which the mediums communicate with the dead is called a séance.

The first—and among the best-known mediums—were three sisters from New York, Margaret and Kate Fox and their much-older sister, Leah Fox Fish. For more than thirty years beginning around 1850, one or more of these women conducted numerous séances. People seated around a table in a dark room would ask questions that the "spirits" would answer with knocks. For example, one knock could mean yes, two knocks no. Sometimes the knocks would be heard from under the table; sometimes they would seem to come from a wall or door. Some people claimed to have "exposed" the sisters, although a number of skeptics tried, without success, to explain how the knocking was produced. In 1888 Margaret Fox finally confessed—though later recanted—that the séances had been a hoax. She demonstrated how she and her sisters could make knocking sounds by snapping the last joint of their big toes. Knocks on doors and walls were made by slipping a foot from a shoe and sliding the foot against a door or a wall before snapping the toe.

Perhaps the most famous medium was Mina "Margery" Crandon, wife of a Boston surgeon, who was active in the 1920s. She claimed to speak through the voice of her deceased brother. During her séances there was ghostly music, rattling chains, levitating chairs, stools, and tables, as well as the deep profanity-filled voice of her dead brother. James Bird, associate editor of *Scientific American*, and an investigating

Harry Houdini (1874–1926) was the world's greatest escape artist. He exposed many fraudulent mediums who claimed to have supernatural powers.

committee commissioned by the magazine were very impressed by Margery. In fact, they were ready to award her the $2,500 prize that had been offered to anyone who could demonstrate that he or she possessed psychic ability. Before the prize was awarded, the world-famous magician Harry Houdini asked to attend one of her séances. Although some observers claimed that Houdini resorted to trickery to expose Margery, she became discredited in the eyes of most people.

During the séance Houdini sat on Margery's left; her husband sat on her right. Adjacent hands and legs were touching all the way around the table. But Houdini discovered that Margery moved her leg so her foot could touch a button on top of a box that caused a bell inside the box to ring. He showed how she could toss a megaphone across the room with a quick twist of her head. She had placed the megaphone, he said, on her head after the lights were turned off and before hands were joined. With his left hand, Houdini reached under the table and found Margery using her head to lift the table, making it appear to "levitate." At a following séance Houdini placed a box he had made around Margery. All psychic phenomena ceased. The committee voted 4–1 not to award the money to Margery. The dissenting vote came from Bird, who was still convinced Margery had psychic powers.

Later, others were again—or still—convinced of Margery's psychic ability when she revealed a fingerprint of her dead brother during a séance. How a spirit could leave a fingerprint is not clear. Certainly the print did not belong to anyone at the séance. Several years later it was discovered that it matched one from the hand of Margery's dentist.

With regard to mediums, the words of Houdini are prophetic: "Anyone can talk to the dead, but the dead do not answer." Rose Mackenberg, who worked with Houdini in exposing mediums, continued their work after Houdini's death. She said marriages must be made in heaven because, although she had never married, mediums had conveyed 1,500 messages to her from departed "husbands and sons." Not one of them ever had the psychic ability to recognize that she was a debunker of their profession, a person who demonstrated on stage how tables, trumpets, and megaphones could be made to levitate, how sealed messages could be read, and how ectoplasm (fleshlike tissue, supposedly from a spirit) could emerge during a séance.

Activity 10 in Chapter 4 shows you how to conduct a séance in which a number of people are seated around a table in the dark. Activity 11 in that chapter is a séance in which a Ouija board is used.

CHAPTER
three

UFOs and Extraterrestrials

o you—like many other people—believe that UFOs exist and that they carry aliens (extraterrestrial beings) from worlds light-years away? While most scientists think there is no convincing evidence that UFOs or aliens have landed on Earth, many of them do believe that communication with intelligent extraterrestrial beings may be possible.

SETI

One thing on which most scientists agree is that attempts to communicate with us by other forms of intelligent life light-years away would not be by space vehicles. Sending vehicles through space requires so much energy and time that no intelligent beings would use them when they could send radio waves, which require far less energy and travel at the maximum speed possible—the velocity of light. The recent discovery of at least three planets orbiting stars within our galaxy provides additional hope that extraterrestrial life may exist. Since there are other solar systems—planets orbiting a star like our sun—it is possible that the conditions necessary for life exist elsewhere in our vast universe.

The Search for Extraterrestrial Intelligence (SETI) involves several different programs. One of them consists of a huge dishlike radio telescope 84 feet (25.6 meters) in diameter near Harvard University. It scans the sky over the Northern Hemisphere. A similar instrument at the Argentine Institute of Radio Astronomy surveys the southern sky. If an unnatural-appearing signal is detected, the telescope will return to its position in the sky and collect more data.

Of course, no one knows for certain what wave frequency an alien intelligence would use. That is why the telescope searches a wide range. Many astronomers think that any intelligent beings seeking a response would transmit pulses at a frequency or frequencies between 1,000 and 10,000 megahertz (cycles per second). The reason for this is that there are relatively few other "noises" in this frequency range traveling through space. What information might we find in such a signal? Perhaps the simple repetition of a prime number; a language encoded and taught in successive lessons; or binary digits that, when arranged properly in rows and columns, would provide recognizable patterns or pictures.

As we search for signals from distant civilizations, we continue to direct our own radio pulses toward regions in space where we think life might exist. A number of attempts to communicate with extraterrestrials have been made, but no answers have been received, at least none that have been detected.

UFOs

Although reports of unidentified flying objects have been reported throughout history, the most recent series began in 1947. On June 24 pilot Kenneth Arnold reported seeing nine objects traveling at about 1,000 miles (1,600 kilometers) per hour near Mount Rainier, Washington.

He said they "flew like they take a saucer and throw it across the water." From the press came the term "flying saucers," and people have been finding saucer-shaped objects in the sky ever since.

There is no conclusive evidence that spacecraft from another world occupy our skies or have landed on our soil. However, there are enough reports of viewings by people of sound mind to make some scientists believe that such extraterrestrial vehicles may exist and that we should try to find them. Indeed, if they exist, scientists would be eager to examine them and to talk with those who fly them. Furthermore, we would expect such aliens to seek out and try to communicate with astronomers and other scientists who are

Figure 3 Is this an alien from the planet Hoova?

best qualified to understand them and their mission. The fact that they don't seek such people makes their existence even more questionable.

In addition to reported sightings and landings of saucer-shaped spaceships from another world, there are numerous accounts of people who claim they have been kidnapped by aliens. These beings from afar are said to look like the one shown in Figure 3. The aliens usually bring their victims to a spaceship, where they are examined, sometimes lectured. Then they carry the victims back to the place from which they were abducted.

Was this debris found near Roswell, New Mexico, the remains of a UFO or a fallen radar balloon that was part of a top-secret military project?

The Roswell Incident

There are many stories about, and sightings of, flying saucers. Perhaps the most widely discussed incident is one that occurred near Roswell, New Mexico, in 1947. UFO enthusiasts say that two extraterrestrial spaceships (flying saucers) collided in a thunderstorm. Personnel from the Roswell Army Air Field were informed of the event by a local rancher who discovered the widely spread debris. The air force reported that a weather balloon had crashed at the site. The rancher said later that he had picked up some of the debris. It included pieces of a gray, smoky, rubbery material; sticks; tinfoil; eyelets; aluminum rings; strange-looking pieces of metal with hieroglyphic-like markings; and a black box.

Thirty years later, witnesses claimed that the debris and four aliens killed in the crash had been transferred to an air force base in Ohio, where a secret study was conducted. A Roswell mortician said he had seen some of the wreckage and had been asked to supply sealed caskets. He was told to remain silent about what he had seen. The mortician said that a nurse he knew, who later disappeared, told him she had helped doctors examine the hairless bodies of three creatures about two-thirds human size. They had huge heads, deep-set eyes, tiny ears, and black skin.

According to many people, the incident was covered up by the government and kept secret by top-echelon members of the armed forces, the CIA, and the National Security Council. In 1984 Jamie Shandera, a film producer interested in UFOs, found a canister of film in his mailbox. When the film was developed, it turned out to be a series of secret papers issued on September 24, 1947, by then-President Harry S Truman. Known as the MJ–12 documents, they contained references to appendices (which were missing) giving details about UFOs and aliens. The papers indicated that Truman established a committee of twelve scientists and government officials (the Majestic Twelve) to look into crashed flying saucers and alien bodies that had been discovered. Experts who examined the documents said they were a hoax. Truman's signature was identical to his signature on another letter, but magnified by 3.6 percent.

No one's signature is ever identical to a previous one. A 3.6 percent increase in size indicates the signature was copied three times, because xerographic copies are enlarged by 1.2 percent. Furthermore, the document was written on a typewriter that was not available before 1963.

In 1993 the air force finally revealed that what fell to Earth near Roswell was not merely a weather balloon but a top-secret radar balloon, part of a program called Project Mogul. Information provided by Charles B. Moore, one of the scientists who worked on Project Mogul, supports the air force account. Project Mogul's goal was to monitor nuclear explosions in the Soviet Union by placing microphones at very high altitudes. The microphones were carried to these altitudes by a train of as many as twenty-four helium balloons having a total length greater than 600 feet (183 meters). In June and July 1947 trial flights of these balloons were being launched from the Alamogordo Army Air Field in New Mexico.

Moore's description of the materials used in the balloons matches well with the debris described at the site. The balloons were made of neoprene (a synthetic rubber) and would have melted into the gray rubbery matter described by the rancher. The radar reflectors used to track the balloons were made of sticks, thin metallic sheets ("tinfoil"), and the strangely marked tape. The radar targets had small eyelets similar to those found in the debris, and aluminum rings 3 inches (7.6 centimeters) in diameter were used to launch the balloons. Moore remembered that the tape used on the radar targets had a variety of curious, hieroglyphic-like markings because it was purchased from a toy factory. Batteries to power the microphones were packed in black boxes. A study of weather reports of that area for early June indicate that a flight called NYU Flight 4, consisting of weather balloons, launched on June 4, 1947, would have been carried by winds to the site where the wreckage was later discovered. Radar trackers lost contact with the flight a few miles from the crash site.

In 1995, following an eighteen-month search requested by Congressman Steve Schiff of New Mexico, the government's General Accounting Office found no evidence to refute the air force's account of the Roswell incident. The search included a review of the classified minutes of the meetings of the National Security Council (NSC) for 1947 and 1948. These minutes contained no mention of the Roswell incident. It seems highly likely that if a flying saucer had crashed and aliens had been found, the NSC would have discussed it. Indeed, if such an event really did occur, it seems very unlikely that it could have been kept secret for fifty years.

In the summer of 1997 a report by a CIA historian indicated that the public had been deliberately misled on a large percentage of the UFO sightings reported during the 1950s and 60s.

Aliens and an Autopsy

In the March/April 1997 issue of *Skeptical Inquirer*, astronomer Alan Hale states, "Extraordinary claims require extraordinary evidence." As an astronomer, he has spent much of his life watching the sky without ever seeing an object that is not part of the natural world. He goes on to argue that if he is to believe that aliens have landed on Earth, he would like to see and, if possible, talk to one.

About eighteen months earlier, on August 28, 1995, the Fox Television Network broadcast "Alien Autopsy: Fact or Fiction?" reportedly showing an autopsy performed on one of the dead aliens discovered at the Roswell site. Apparently, Hale did not accept the alien autopsy shown in the program as convincing evidence. Indeed, most viewers found that the question raised in the film's title was easily answered. A pathologist and others who saw the film noted these things: There was no body block (a device used by pathologists to raise the trunk and head). The "surgeon" seen in the film used his scissors as might a tailor but certainly not a surgeon. The surgical gowns worn by the "doctors" offered no protection from germs, odor, or possible radiation. The organs removed from the alien's abdomen bore no resemblance to actual internal organs and were removed without cutting away any of the connective tissue that normally holds them in place. The procedure did not follow the usual pattern used by pathologists. And finally, the features of the alien shown in the film—medium-size body, small ears, five fingers, and a thumb—did not match those described by observers at Roswell who said the aliens were small and earless, with hands that had four fingers and no thumbs.

In an article entitled "How to Make an 'Alien' for 'Autopsy,'" which can be found in the January/February 1996 issue of *Skeptical Inquirer*, Trey Stokes, a professional special-effects artist, explains how the alien could have been made and the autopsy faked. He concludes that two possibilities exist: (1) The film is an authentic autopsy of a real alien that looks just like a special-effects creature and was filmed in Hollywood fashion, omitting details that cover the flaws in the procedure. (2) The film is a fake autopsy using a special-effects creature.

Stokes concludes that without more evidence the second option is far more likely.

Immediately following Stokes's article is a piece ("A Surgeon's View: Alien Autopsy's Overwhelming Lack of Credibility") by Joseph A. Bauer, M.D. After detailing the totally unprofessional nature of the autopsy as filmed, Bauer concludes that either the film is a hoax, or it reveals the destruction of the valuable evidence needed to gain some understanding of the alien creature being examined.

Aliens and UFOs

Reports of being kidnapped by aliens are not uncommon; however, many people seem to be able to recall the experience only when hypnotized. The experiences reported by those who claim to have been abducted share many common features: It's dark, you're in bed, you sense that you are paralyzed. You see one or more small gray beings near the bed. They have bald, pear-shaped heads with large, totally black eyes. They carry you through the walls of your room to a saucer-shaped ship, which you sometimes enter by riding up a light beam. Inside the ship are bright lights and a table on which they examine your paralyzed body. They may extract eggs or sperm cells and insert devices into your brain through your nose or ear. Sometimes they give you a telepathic lecture—they don't speak—on a social problem such as our failure to properly care for the environment, AIDS, or some other issue confronting society. Later you are in bed and may remember nothing until you hear of someone who had a similar experience or you recall the experience under hypnosis or in a dream.

A few of those who report such abductions are probably hoaxers, but there are too many reports for that to explain all of them. Some people who have investigated reports of alien abductions believe they really do occur. (See *Intruders: The Incredible Visitations at Copley Woods* by Budd Hopkins.) Most scientists refuse to accept the existence of aliens and spaceships from other worlds without more tangible proof. They look for more believable causes.

In *The Demon-Haunted World*, Carl Sagan suggested that alien abductions are delusions that may result from sleep paralysis. During active dreams our muscles are often paralyzed, an adaptation that prevents us from hurting ourselves while asleep. In that twilight state between being asleep and awake, many people experience effects similar to those reported by people who say they were abducted—paralysis, rapid heart rate, a feeling that they have a weight on their chests, seeing a bright light. During this fearful state of paralysis, people often have hallucinations that seem real. The similarity in the reports of people supposedly abducted by aliens suggests a physiological response like near-death experiences. People revived after nearly dying all report seeing a bright white light and feeling a sense of bliss. Many physicians believe it to be the brain's response to a lack of oxygen.

Several decades ago, Wilder Penfield, a Canadian neurophysiologist, found that electrical stimulation of a person's brain can produce real-appearing hallucinations. They include anxiety, a sense of floating, the presence of strange beings, and a suspension of time. Such reactions are common among people with temporal lobe epilepsy, in which a vast number of electrical impulses are released simultaneously in a region along the side of the brain. In at least one case, carbamazepine, an antiepileptic drug, eliminated recurring alien abduction experiences.

Mass hallucinations are not uncommon. Around the turn of the twentieth century, after Percival Lowell claimed that Mars was covered with a network of canals, many people reported encounters with Martians. After *Mariner 9*, in 1971, failed to detect any canals on Mars and *Viking 1* and *Viking 2*, in 1976, found the planet to be without life, reports of encounters with Martians declined. But reports of other aliens had existed. George Adamski, who operated a small restaurant at the base of Mount Palomar, California, in the 1950s, claimed he had talked with aliens from Venus. After space probes sent to Venus in the 1970s revealed that its surface temperature was about 900°F (500°C), enthusiasm for Adamski's aliens faded.

Neuroscientist Michael Persinger believes that alien-abduction scenarios and other mystical experiences are associated with abnormal nerve activity in the temporal lobes of the brain, the same region that affects those with temporal lobe epilepsy. Furthermore, he thinks that abnormal activity there can be brought on by changes in Earth's magnetic field. He has found a link between earthquakes, which produce magnetic changes, and the incidence of UFO sightings, reports of alien abductions, and other strange phenomena. To test his idea, Persinger produces changing magnetic fields using electrical coils in a helmet that his subjects wear as they lie in a reclining chair. Some people who have taken part in the experiment say they feel as if they are swaying, being held by the shoulders, and having their legs stretched. They become disoriented. Some also report emotional effects such as anger, fear, and weakness. While such results do not offer proof of Persinger's hypothesis, they do suggest that changing magnetic fields can affect the brain and produce hallucinogenic effects.

Crop Circles

In 1976 people in England began to notice circles impressed in fields of grain. When viewed from above, the circles appeared to be perfectly shaped. From year to year, the designs became more complex. Concentric circles appeared, circles connected by an axis or by parallel lines, smaller

Were these elaborate designs in English grain fields the work of aliens trying to communicate with earthlings or were they the work of hoaxers?

circles tangent to a larger one, circles with small designs attached so that the figure resembled a musical note or the symbol for male or female, and so on. (See the photo on page 41.) By 1990 the letters *DD* began to appear, and a message written in trampled wheat read, "WE ARE NOT ALONE."

Several scientists claimed that the crop circles and designs could not have been made by humans, but they were at a loss to explain their origins. People became convinced that an alien culture on board UFOs was making the symbols in an effort to communicate with earthlings.

In 1991 two Englishmen, Doug Bower and Dave Chorley, confessed that crop circles were a hoax they had dreamed up one evening as they chatted at their pub, the Percy Hobbes. As the press made more and more of the circles, they began making more elaborate designs. The letters *DD* that appeared in 1990 stood for Doug and Dave; they had begun to sign their work. The "WE ARE NOT ALONE" message was in response to the work of some copycat hoaxers who had also begun to make designs in grainfields. Bower and Chorley showed reporters how they used a steel bar, planks, and ropes to flatten the grain. Their confession drew only modest press; readers preferred the excitement of an extraterrestrial explanation.

Making crop circles is not suggested. But if you would like to make your own mysterious snow circles some winter evening, see Activity 14 in Chapter 4.

CHAPTER four

Experimenting with Paranormal Phenomena

In the first three chapters of this book you read about a number of paranormal phenomena. Now you can examine some of these topics more directly by carrying out some hands-on activities.

Activities 1–8 in this chapter involve examining ESP and PK. After doing these experiments, you can make up your own mind about whether people possess these paranormal powers.

In Activity 9, you will carry out an analysis to see how Randi explained the thought photographs discussed in Chapter 1. Activities 10 and 11 involve séances: an around-the-table séance with levitation and a Ouija board séance. Activity 12 shows how you can make someone think he or she is being touched by a spirit. Finally, Activity 13 suggests a way to make not crop circles but snow circles.

ACTIVITY 1
Testing for ESP with Zener Cards

You will need:
- 2 packs of Zener cards (25 in each deck).
  You may be able to buy these cards in a store that
  sells occult items, or you can make your own,
  as shown in Figure 5.

    To do this you will need:
    - white file cards (3 x 5 inches)
    - sheets of paper 8 1/2 x 11 inches
    - a copier
    - scissors

- comfortable room
- card table
- another small table
- 2 chairs
- an opaque (lightproof) screen, curtain, or wall
  between the two tables
- lined paper
- pencil

If you can't buy a deck of Zener cards, you can create your own by using a copier to make five copies of the drawings found in Figure 4. Glue or tape these five different figures to the twenty-five file cards, as shown in Figure 5. (Note: Be sure that there are no irregularities in the cards that will allow a subject to identify a card even when it is facedown.)

Two people, the sender and the receiver, or subject, are seated at small tables on opposite sides of a large opaque screen, curtain, or wall. The subject—the person who will attempt to receive the thoughts of the sender—has a pencil or pen and a ruled sheet of paper, set up like the one shown in the chart opposite. This chart should extend down to number 25.

FIGURE 4 You can make Zener cards like these and use them to find out whether or not people have ESP.

FIGURE 5 Glue the 5 different symbols to 3 x 5" file cards to make a deck of 25 cards. The deck should contain 5 cards of each symbol.

	SYMBOL ON CARD				
Card Number	circle	cross	star	square	squiggly line
1	✔				
2					
3					
. . . . .					
. . . . .					

The sender spreads the cards, face down, over the table and mixes them up. If you are the sender attempting to transmit the symbol by ESP, you turn up a card and stare at it for a maximum of thirty seconds. During that time, try to avoid all other thoughts. At the moment the card is turned over, you will say, "Card number one: Go!" This tells the second person (the receiver) seated at a table on the other side of the large opaque screen, curtain, or wall to begin concentrating on the thought (the symbol) that the sender is trying to transmit by telepathy.

When the subject thinks she knows the symbol, she makes a check mark under the proper column beside the number 1. (In the chart above, the subject thought the first card carried a circle and recorded it as shown.) After the subject checks the symbol she thinks is on the card, she says, "Okay!" If, after thirty seconds, the subject has not responded, the sender says, "Time!" and places the card facedown at one corner of the table. If the subject does not think she knows the symbol on the card at which the sender has been staring, she simply leaves the row next to the number blank. The sender turns up a second card, says, "Card number two: Go!" and the process is repeated. This continues until all twenty-five cards have been turned over and stacked in order at the corner of the sender's table. Use a paper clip or rubber band to secure the cards in the order they were drawn.

If both sender and subject do not feel tired or bored at the end of the first trial, they can repeat the experiment using a second deck of thoroughly shuffled or mixed cards. To avoid confusion, attach a card with a large 1 on it to the first deck and mark the receiver's chart with the same number. If either person feels tired or unable to concentrate, delay additional trials.

To eliminate bias from the analysis, it is best if two people who were not present during the experiment analyze the data. One person looks at the cards in the order they were turned over and announces the symbols on those cards in proper order to the second person. The second person looks at the symbols that were checked on the chart by the subject (receiver). If the symbol checked by the subject matches the one on the card, it is called a "hit," and the check mark is circled.

At the end of the analysis, count the number of circled checks (hits) and write that number at the bottom of the chart. You would expect a subject to correctly identify 5 of the 25, or 20 percent of the cards because she has a 1 in 5 chance of being right just by guessing. Consistent scores well above 20 percent, such as 9 out of 25 (36 percent), may indicate a person with ESP. What do scores below 20 percent suggest?

Try to do as many trials as possible, and test as many people as you can. Be sure to keep the data for each subject and sender pair separate from all other pairs. Does any of your data suggest a subject and sender who seem to have ESP? If you find such a pair, try to run additional tests to see if their success continues over many trials. If you find someone who appears to have ESP, ask a mathematics teacher to figure out the odds of that person scoring so well.

ACTIVITY 2
Testing for ESP with Playing Cards

You will need:
- A pack of ordinary playing cards
- comfortable room
- card table
- another small table
- two chairs
- an opaque screen or curtain between the two tables

- lined paper
- pencil

You can do a similar experiment to test for ESP using an ordinary deck of cards. First, remove the aces. This will leave you with forty-eight cards, twelve in each suit. Shuffle the deck well and place the cards facedown on the table. Turn the first card faceup and focus your eyes on it as you did with the Zener cards while your subject on the other side of the screen tries to receive your signal—heart, diamond, spade, or club—and records his choice with a check mark on a chart similar to the one used in Activity 1.

In this case, the subject's chances for choosing the same suit that you are looking at is 1 in 4, or 25 percent, because there are only four choices. Try to go through the cards five times, shuffling thoroughly before each trial. Of course, you don't have to do all five trials at one session. The subject in this experiment can be expected to score 60 hits by chance alone (1/4 x 48 x 5 = 60). Significantly higher scores, 90 for example, would indicate the subject may have ESP. Is there evidence of ESP if sender and subject switch roles?

How could you redesign this experiment to test yourself for clairvoyance? That is, to see if you know the suit of the card on top of the deck? How could you avoid bias in analyzing your results?

ACTIVITY 3
Testing for ESP With Picture Postcards

You will need:
- 5 brightly colored picture postcards each with completely different scenes—a lighthouse, a sunset, a baseball game, etc.
- aluminum foil
- 5 opaque envelopes that can be sealed
- comfortable room
- table
- chair

- subjects
- pad and pencil

Obtain five different brightly colored picture postcards. Wrap each one in aluminum foil and place it in its own opaque envelope. Seal and number the envelopes.

Ask a subject to sit at a table on which you have placed the sealed envelopes. Then ask the subject to use her ESP to create a mental image of the picture inside each numbered envelope. Ask her to write the number of the envelope on the pad and then words to describe her vision of the picture inside. Be sure not to give any clues as to the nature of the postcards. Simply tell the subject that each envelope contains a picture postcard and that she is to try to describe the picture using ESP.

Record the subject's name on the sheet of paper she used to describe the picture. After you have tested a number of subjects, you might invite them all back for the grand opening of the envelopes. Don't be surprised if some of the subjects claim their descriptions were hits even if you are convinced that they weren't.

Another way to do this experiment is to give the subjects a pencil and colored pens. Then ask them to sketch the pictures they think are on each postcard. Regardless of which method you use, did any of the subjects appear to have ESP?

ACTIVITY 4
Testing for Transfer of Images by ESP

You will need:
- pad and pencil
- comfortable room
- 2 small tables and 2 chairs
- an opaque screen or curtain between the two tables

Sit at a table and concentrate on drawing a picture of something that is not in the room. It might be a car, a boat, a house, or a landscape. On the other side of an opaque screen, a subject sitting at another table tries to receive a message from you by ESP. Based on the message, she tries to draw a picture similar to the one you are making.

A similar experiment can be done sitting quietly in a chair and focusing on a picture, a painting, or a photograph. At the same time, a subject on the other side of the opaque screen tries to pick up the images in your mind and record them on paper by means of words or a sketch.

Repeat several times whichever procedure you use. Be sure that both you and your subject place corresponding numbers on each of the drawings and records that were done at the same time. How closely do the pictures you drew or focused on match those drawn or recorded by your subject? Is there any evidence that information was transmitted by ESP? If you switch roles (sender and subject), is there evidence of ESP?

ACTIVITY 5
Mental Telepathy and Your Pet

You will need:
- pad and pencil
- comfortable room
- 2 small tables and 2 chairs
- an opaque screen or curtain between the two tables

Some people claim that telepathic messages between animals and humans are possible. If you have a pet, you might try to test such claims.

If your pet is a dog or a cat that freely moves about your home, try to send it a message from a different room. To help you relax, sit quietly, take a deep breath, hold it for a count of three, and then slowly exhale. Repeat this three times. Then close your eyes. Focus your mind on an image of your pet. Once you have a good image of your pet, form another image of the message you want to send. For example, tell your pet through telepathy that you would like it to come to you within the next five minutes. Continue to focus on your pet and that message for that period of time. Does the animal respond to your telepathic message?

If your pet responds, it doesn't necessarily mean you established telepathic communication. Can you repeat the experiment? With the same conditions, sit in the same room and read so that your mind is focused on the ideas in a book or magazine and not on your pet. What does it mean if your pet still comes to you after a few minutes? What does it mean if it doesn't come to you?

Here's another experiment to try. After doing some deep-breathing exercises to relax, move to a position some distance behind your pet when it is resting. Then concentrate on the back of the pet's head and try to communicate through telepathy that you would like it to turn around and look at you. Does your pet respond within five minutes? What else should you do to be sure that telepathy and not just your presence over time caused the animal to respond?

If you think you have established a telepathic link with a dog that is trained to fetch objects, you might like to try this more difficult experiment. Sit at a table some distance behind your dog. Use a pencil or pen to make a drawing of a ball, a stick, a bone, or some other object the dog could carry to you. Concentrate on the drawing for several minutes. Then, after several deep breaths to make you relax, try to send the image to your dog by telepathy for several minutes. Repeat the relaxation exercises before you try to communicate to the dog through telepathy that you want it to fetch the object you have drawn.

Does your pet respond within five minutes? What else should you do to be sure that telepathy and not something else is responsible for the animal's response?

ACTIVITY 6
Testing for PK Power by Rolling a Die

You will need:
- die
- small tin can
- pad of paper and pencil

To carry out one test for psychokinesis, place a die (half of a pair of dice) in a small tin can. Shake the die in the can and then roll it out onto the floor. The top face of the six-faced cubic die will show a number of dots from 1 to 6. To test your PK power, choose the number (1, 2, 3, 4, 5, or 6) that you will try to make come up on the top die face. Assuming the die is uniform, what is the probability that the top face of the rolling die will have one dot? That it will have two dots? Three dots? Four? Five? Six?

Tell a friend the number of dots that you are going to try to use PK power to make appear more than can be expected according to chance. Then begin shaking and rolling the die. To avoid bias, your friend will determine the number of dots on the die's top face and record it each time you roll the die. Roll the die at least a hundred times.

According to chance, what fraction of the rolls should have the number you chose? What fraction of the rolls you made came up with the number you were trying to make appear by PK? Is there evidence that you have PK power? If you think there is, continue to try to influence the die in another series of rolls. Is there still evidence of PK? Let your friend test for his or her PK power. Does your friend seem to have PK power?

Design an experiment to see if you can use PK to influence whether a coin turns up heads or tails. What do you find? Can you use PK to make a pendulum start swinging without touching it?

ACTIVITY 7
PK With Your Own Fingers

You will need:
- your own hands

After clasping your two hands tightly together, extend your two index fingers, as shown in Figure 6. Try to keep them about half an inch (13 mm) apart. Meanwhile, using your PK power, focus on the two fingers and silently tell them to come together.

If your two fingers do finally meet, do you think it was due to PK or muscle fatigue? What makes you think so?

52

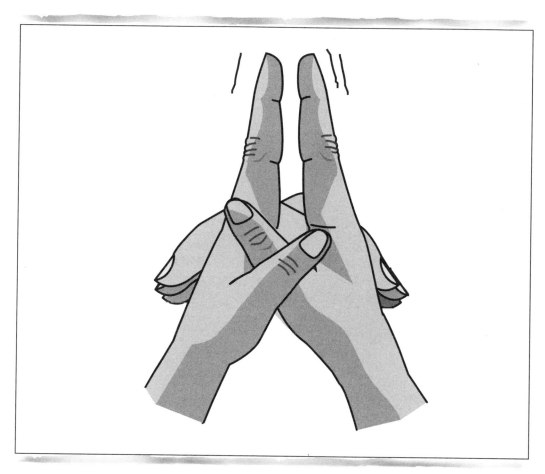

FIGURE 6 Try to keep your extended index fingers apart while consciously directing them to come together.

ACTIVITY **8**
The Swinging Pendulum

You will need:
- finger ring
- thread
- glass tumbler
- tape

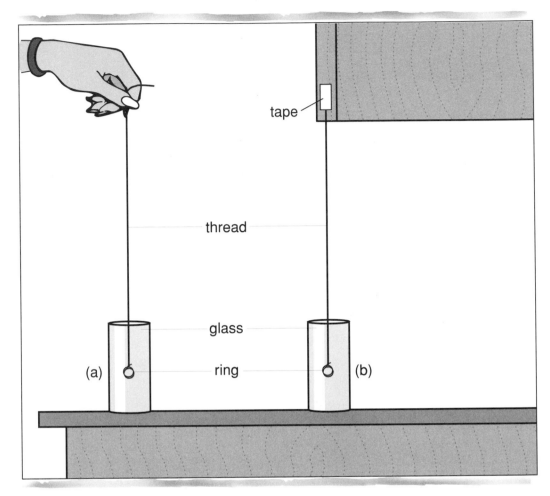

FIGURE 7 a) Suspend the ring from a thread so that it becomes the bob of a pendulum. You hold the top of the thread in your hand. The ring is inside a glass tumbler. b) Now the pendulum is suspended from the front of a chair or a cabinet over a kitchen counter. You are not touching the thread or ring, which is again inside a glass.

A pendulum consists of a small weight, called a bob, that is suspended from a string or a thread attached to a support. You can make a small pendulum by tying a piece of thread about 2 feet (60 centimeters) long to a ring from your finger—or someone else's. Hold the ring, suspended from the thread, at the center of a drinking glass, as shown in Figure 7a. Now, concentrate your attention on the ring. As you watch the ring, think of a number between 1 and 10. The ring will soon begin to swing like a pendulum. The length of the swings will slowly increase until the ring strikes the glass. You might have PK if whatever number you choose, the ring strikes the glass exactly that number of times. If you chose the number 5, the ring should strike the glass five times and then stop!

If you found that you were able to will the ring to swing and strike the glass a certain number of times, there are two possibilities: (1) you have PK power; or (2) unconscious muscular action set the ring to swinging and striking the glass.

To find out which of the two possibilities is probably responsible, tape the top end of the thread to which the ring is attached to a chair or cabinet, as shown in Figure 7b, so that the ring hangs nearly motionless in the center of the glass. If you really have PK power, you should be able to make the ring swing and strike the side of the glass a number of times equal to the number on which you are concentrating. Try it! What do you conclude?

ACTIVITY 9
The Making of Thought Photographs

You will need:
- magnifying lens with a short focal length, about 2 inches (5 centimeters)
- ruler
- cardboard tube about 1 1/2 inches (4 centimeters) in diameter
- scissors
- an old photo slide, 2 x 2 inches (5 x 5 centimeters)

(Note: This is a somewhat difficult activity, so persevere.)

To see how a "thought" photograph can be made, you can make a somewhat larger version of the tube James Randi held against the TV camera.

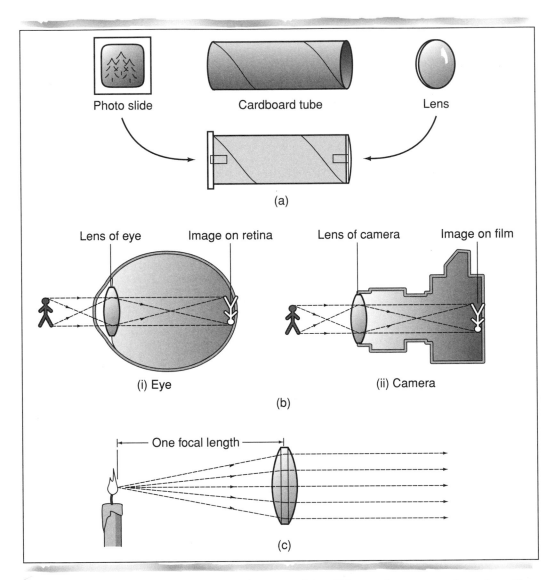

FIGURE 8 a) A cardboard tube, a photographic slide, and a convex lens together with a camera are used to make "thought" photographs. **b)** The lens of the human eye (i) and the lens of a camera (ii) both produce images. In the eye, the images form on the retina, in the camera, the images are formed on film. **c)** Light rays from points one focal length from a lens will be parallel after passing through the lens.

You will need a convex (magnifying) lens with a short focal length. To find the focal length, stand near a white wall on the opposite side of the room from a window that faces an open space. Move the lens closer and farther from the wall. At some point you will find that a clear upside-down image of some distant object seen through the window appears on the wall. Use a ruler to measure the distance between the lens and the image on the wall. That distance is the focal length of the lens.

Next, you will need a cardboard tube. (The tube from a roll of toilet paper is good.) Use scissors to cut the tube so it has the same length as the focal length of the lens. Tape the lens to one end of the tube. Tape a 2 x 2-inch (5 x 5-centimeter) photographic slide of some colorful scene to the other end as shown in Figure 8a. Instead of a camera, you can use your eye, which behaves much like a camera. The lens in your eye forms an image on the eye's retina in the same way that a camera forms an image on the film at the back of the camera. (See Figure 8b.)

If the lens is one focal length from the slide, the light rays coming from any point on the slide will be parallel after they pass through the lens, as shown in Figure 8c. Therefore, the light rays entering the camera's lens will be similar to light rays from a distant object.

Hold the tube in front of your eye. The end of the tube with the lens should be next to your eye. The other end of the tube to which the slide is taped should face a window or a light. What do you see when you look through the tube? What image would form on a camera lens?

By using a lens with a very short focal length and a tiny slide, a thought photographer can hide the tube that holds these devices between his thumb and index finger.

ACTIVITY 10
Touched by a Spirit

You will need:
- a friend
- your own hands

Tell a friend that she will be touched by a spirit. Hold your two index fingers in front of your seated friend's eyes. Say to your friend, "Close your eyes while I press my two fingers gently against them." Once your friend's eyes are closed, hold the index and middle finger of *one* hand, not the index fingers of two, against her eyes. You now have one hand free to touch your friend on the ear, the side of the neck, the back of the head. . . . Then move your free hand back to where it was so that when your friend opens her eyes she again sees your two extended index fingers.

ACTIVITY **11**
Snow Circles

You will need:
- a friend
- length of rope or clothesline
- snow-covered field

In England two men made crop circles. If you live where it snows, you can make snow circles. On a moonlight night, put on your boots, grab a length of rope or clothesline to serve as a radius for your circles, and ask a friend to join you in stomping out circles and other designs in a large snow-covered field. Some hieroglyphiclike symbols will enhance your hoax. How can you hide your tracks leading to the snow circles?

Does anyone notice your designs? Does anyone suspect aliens are responsible?

ACTIVITY **12**
Ouija Board Séance

You will need:
- several friends
- Ouija board

The Ouija board, originally called "Ouija Talking Board," was invented by William Fuld about a hundred years ago. Parker Brothers is the current manufacturer.

Ouija Board

You and a friend place your fingertips on a Ouija board's planchette—
a three-legged, heart-shaped message indicator. When you ask questions
of the board, the planchette moves, as if guided by some spirit, spelling
out answers. After you have obtained some answers from the board, try
answering the next few questions while both of you look not at the
board but at the ceiling. Have one unbiased observer record the answers

spelled out by the planchette while a second observer makes sure that neither of you looks down at the board.

If a spirit is guiding the planchette, where the questioners look should have no effect. However, if the planchette moves because of unconscious muscular movements that produce desired answers, then the results obtained when participants look at the ceiling may be meaningless gibberish. What do the results of your experiment indicate?

ACTIVITY 13
Séance Events

You will need:
- three friends
- lightweight card table
- totally dark room
- slate
- chalk

Have three friends sit with you around a lightweight card table in a totally dark room. Place your hands at the corners of the table so that the tips of your little fingers touch the tips of the little fingers of those on your right and left. Tell your friends that you feel spirits are in the room. Ask them to make their presence known. If you press the heels of your hands against the edge of the table, it will tilt. By slipping your thumbs under the edge of the table you can lift it. If your friend on the other side of the table is in on your little hoax, the two of you can make the table levitate (rise off the floor). If you can slip the edges of the soles of your shoes under the table legs, you can lift the table by yourself. Just lift your feet as you apply pressure with the heels of your hands and the table will levitate. If you are as agile as Margery, the Boston Medium, you may be able to lift the table with your head.

You might place a blank slate under the table and ask the spirit to leave a message. During the séance you could slide the slate under your chair with your foot so that another friend hiding around a corner of the room could remove it and replace it with an identical slate containing some messages scrawled in chalk. Use your foot to slide the new slate under the table.

Finally, design some other activities to enhance the sequence and make it scary. If you can snap your big toe, your spirit can answer all kinds of questions. If not, you can probably tape a remote control to the side of your chest. By pressing your arm against the control you could activate a hidden bell or buzzer that would allow your spirit to provide answers.

CHAPTER five

Mind Reading and Other Psychic Performances

epending on the results of the experiments you did in Chapter 4, you may or may not believe in telepathy. But whether or not telepathy exists makes no difference to people who make a living by "reading" minds. They use tricks to make sure that their "telepathic powers" always work.

In this chapter you can have a lot of fun using your own "supernatural" abilities to amaze and amuse audiences. The telepathic demonstrations you will perform can be done before an audience of any size, although some are best done with a small group. Some of these performances are easy to do; others require practice. You will be able to judge which ones work best for you after you try them. In any case, have fun, and attempt them first with your family or a few friends who promise not to give away your secrets.

SHOW **1**
Mental Telepathy

You will need:
- a partner to serve as a medium
- variety of common objects

Posing as a "psychic," you tell your audience that you believe you can use mental telepathy to transfer their choice of an object to a "medium" (someone with whom you have conspired before the show). With the medium out of the room, the audience chooses an object. When the medium returns, you tell him that the audience has chosen an object and they want to see if the two of you can communicate by mental telepathy by having him identify the object given choices.

You begin to point to various objects while asking each time, "Is it this?" The medium repeatedly responds, "No," until you point to the object the audience chose. At this point, he says, "Yes, that's it!"

THE SECRET
Before the show, you and the medium agreed that you would point to the object chosen by the audience immediately after you pointed to an object of a particular color, such as black. In case the audience requests additional demonstrations, and asks you to indicate the chosen object the first time you point, which is likely, you need an additional signal. You might for example, point with your left hand to alert the medium that the usual signal is off and that he should choose the object you are touching even though you have not yet pointed to anything black.

SHOW **2**
Long-Range Thought Transmission

You will need:
- a partner to serve as a medium
- blindfold
- chair
- common objects such as glasses, coin, pen, etc.
- playing cards

You claim that you have the "psychic" power to transfer thoughts to a blindfolded medium seated nearby. You ask the audience to hold up some objects to be identified, such as coins, rings, watches, glasses, pens, pencils, combs. You then touch someone's glasses, and say, "What am I touching?" The medium responds, "Glass!" Each time you touch something, the medium is able to identify it. Of course, the audience is amazed and many may be convinced that thoughts can be transferred by psychic means.

THE SECRET

Before this act is performed, you and your "medium" must memorize a list of common objects, such as the ones mentioned above, in an agreed-upon order. If the order is glasses, coin, pen, . . . the medium knows that the first item you will choose is a pair of glasses. The second item will be a coin, the third a pen, and so on. A code will also be useful, in case you want to repeat an object in the list. The words very good *might be used to indicate that an item is to be repeated, while all right* could mean an object is to be skipped because it is not available.*

If the audience persists in wanting items identified, you might offer an excuse such as, "A psychic line connecting brains cannot transmit thoughts for very long because it is a very tiring and taxing experience." Or the medium might say that he has lost the intense powers of concentration required to receive messages from another mind.

SHOW 3
Short-Range Thought Transmission

You will need:
- a partner to serve as a psychic
- blindfold
- chair

You ask the audience for a number that your blindfolded "psychic" partner will determine by means of short-range thought transmission. The blindfolded psychic is seated in a chair turned away from the audience.

A member of the audience is invited to indicate a number using fingers on one or both hands so that the psychic can't hear the number. You then sit in the chair while the psychic, still blindfolded, places his fingers gently on your temples, appears to concentrate deeply, and then announces the correct number.

THE SECRET

The number is conveyed to the psychic not by ESP but by your gently contracting your lower jaw muscles. The psychic can feel these contractions. If the number to be transmitted is 4, you contract your jaw muscles four times in rapid succession. If the audience picks a larger number, such as 47, you indicate 4 as before, pause, and then contract your muscles seven times.

SHOW 4
More Mind Reading

You will need:
- a light-skinned volunteer from the audience
- a coin

(Note: This is subtle and may be difficult, so persevere.)

This time you tell your audience that you are going to try the difficult task of reading the mind of someone who is not a medium. You ask for a volunteer from the audience. You choose a light-skinned person from the audience and hand her a coin. You turn away from the volunteer and tell her to place the hand that holds the coin against her forehead while the other hand hangs normally at her side. You ask her to concentrate very hard and try to transfer her thought of the hand holding the coin to you through mental telepathy. You then tell her at the count of three she is to lower the hand with the coin and hold both fists in front of her.

You count to three, turn immediately, and identify the hand that holds the coin. To see whether it was luck or "true" telepathy, you repeat the experiment several times with your first subject and with another volunteer from the audience. Your phenomenal rate of success "proves" that you really do possess psychic powers.

THE SECRET

When you look at the hands of the person who holds the coin, you choose the hand that is paler—the one that has less color. When a person raises his or her arm, blood flow to the hand is reduced, making the skin appear paler.

SHOW 5
It's in the Cards

You will need:
- a partner to serve as a medium
- chair
- playing cards
- table

You claim that you can communicate with a "medium" through ESP. The medium places nine playing cards faceup on a table in a rectangle of three rows, each with three cards, as shown in the photograph Figure 10. The medium is sent from the room. A member of the audience selects a card that you are to communicate to the medium through ESP.

When the medium returns to the room, you point to a card and ask, "Is this the card?" If it is not the card chosen by the audience, the

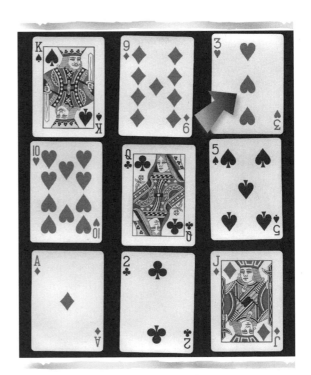

FIGURE 9 What does your "psychic" sense tell you is the card picked by someone from the audience?

66

medium will respond, "No." This is repeated several times until you point to the correct card and the medium responds, "Yes!"

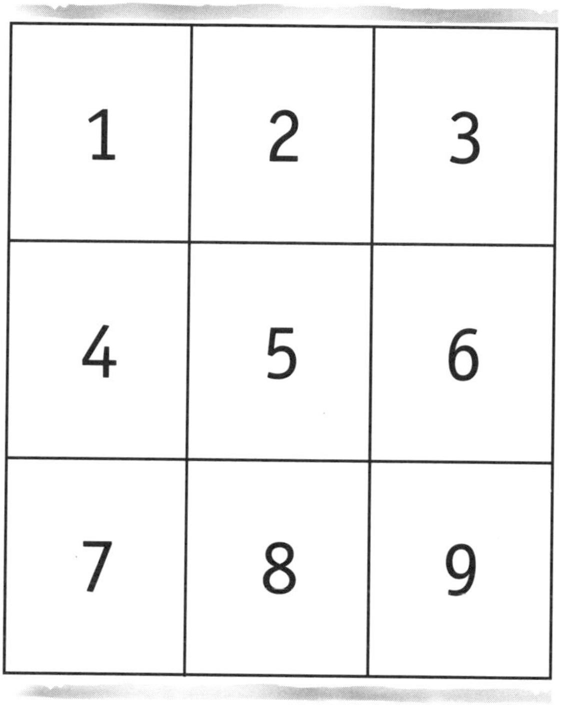

THE SECRET

The correct card is selected not by ESP but by a simple signal. You indicate the card to the medium when you first point to a card. Think of the nine cards as positions on a grid (Figure 11). If your finger touches the upper-right hand corner of the first card you point to, the medium knows that the card in the upper right-hand corner of the nine-card grid (the three of hearts) is the one that was chosen by the

FIGURE 10 The nine cards can be thought of as making up a grid like this one.

audience. If you touch the center of the first card you point to, as is the case in Figure 10, you indicate to the medium that the card at the center of the grid (the queen of clubs) is the correct one. When you finally point to the card that you signaled with your first touch, the medium will respond, "Yes, that's the one!" Of course, the medium must be alert because after several demonstrations the audience may request that your very first point be directed to the card chosen.

SHOW 6
Reading Numbers with Your Mind

You will need:

- a volunteer from the audience
- a table

- pad of paper
- pencil

(Note: This is subtle and may be very difficult to do, so persevere.)

Ask someone to sit at a table with a pencil and a small pad of paper while you stand some distance away. Tell that person to choose a number between 1 and 10. Then tell her to cover the front of the paper with one hand while she writes the number on the paper. Have her fold the paper several times before handing it to you. You place the paper against your forehead, close your eyes, grimace a bit, and then announce the number written on the paper. When the paper is opened, your prediction is confirmed.

THE SECRET

Knowing the number has nothing to do with mind reading and everything to do with careful observation. While the person is writing the number, the paper is shielded from your view, but the top of the pencil is not. By watching the motion of the pencil you can tell what number is being written. Of course, you will have to practice watching someone write numbers a few times before you go on stage with this one. But you will see that it is really quite easy to determine the number that is being written by watching the movement of the pencil.

SHOW 7
Telephonic Telepathy

You will need:
- a volunteer from your audience
- deck of cards
- code of names to identify cards
- telephone partner with code

Ask someone from the audience to select a card from an ordinary deck. Suppose the card is the 3 of spades. You tell the audience that you have a friend who can read minds over the telephone. You look up your friend's number in the telephone book and then ask the volunteer from the audience to call your friend's number and ask for him by name. After your friend answers the phone and confirms his name, you tell the volunteer to ask your friend to identify the card she is holding. Your friend asks her to hold the card against the phone's mouthpiece. He hesitates for a moment and then announces that it is the 3 of spades.

THE SECRET

Before performing this mind-reading feat, you need to prepare a code that you share with a friend you can reach by telephone. The code consists of an alphabetical list of fifty-two names that identifies each card in a deck of playing cards. Part of a code that could be used for a male friend is shown in Table 2.

Table 2: Part of a code used to identify playing cards.

Adam	Ace of spades	*Alphonse*	Five of spades
Alan	Two of spades	*Art*	Six of spades
Albert	Three of spades	*Ben*	Seven of spades
Alex	Four of spades	*Bill*	Eight of spades

A few minutes before the show, call your friend so that he can anticipate a call from someone in your audience. When you pretend to look for your friend's number in the telephone book, you are actually checking the code name for the card selected by the volunteer. If that card was the three of spades, you can see from the code shown in Table 2 that the code name you want is Albert. Since the caller asks for Albert, your friend, who has the code by his phone, immediately knows the volunteer has chosen the three of spades.

If someone asks you to repeat the trick, simply say that Albert has only enough psychic energy to make one identification per day.

SHOW 8
Demonstrating Your Clairvoyant Power

You will need:

- a volunteer from your audience
- paper

- pencil
- book

You can make people think that you have ESP with this simple demonstration. The audience watches you as you write the three words *red*, *chair*, and *rose* on a piece of paper. They can see you writing, but they cannot see the words you wrote. You then place the paper under a book.

You then ask a volunteer from the audience to respond to your requests for a word by saying the word *immediately* after you ask them. Then quickly proceed to ask the following: "Name a color!" Wait for the quick response, then ask: "Name a piece of furniture!" After the response, quickly ask: "Name a flower!"

Finally, show them the words on the paper you placed in the book. It is likely that two or three of their responses will be the words you wrote on the paper.

THE SECRET
The three words you wrote are the most common responses to the requests you ask.

SHOW 9
Seeing Images Via Telepathy

You will need:
- 5 copies of the same magazine
- 4 covers from different issues of the same magazine
- nail file
- stapler

Ask a volunteer from the audience to choose one of five magazines with different covers that you display. You casually pick up one of the remaining four magazines and ask the person to choose a number between, say, 20 and 60. You then ask the person to turn in the magazine she has to the page with that number. Tell your subject to concentrate on the illustration on that page for a few seconds before closing the magazine.

Tell her to try to "see" the illustration in her mind and send you a copy of that image via telepathic "mail." You begin to draw as you pretend to receive pieces of the image. After a minute or so, you might say, "I'm losing the image, would you please take another look and focus on the page for a few seconds."

After the subject opens the magazine and looks at the illustration, you respond, "That's better! It's much clearer now!" as you continue to draw. Once your drawing is finished, ask the subject to describe the illustration on which she concentrated. You then reveal your drawing, which, thanks to the marvels of telepathic communication, closely resembles the image your subject tried to transmit.

If you are a very poor artist, you can write down your "impressions" of the illustration being transmitted instead of making a drawing. You can then recite your impressions before the subject shows the illustration to the audience, or to you if it is a one-on-one session.

THE SECRET

You will need five copies of the same magazine. If possible, choose a magazine with numbered pages that do not include the issue date and one that has lots of illustrations or illustrated advertisements. You will also need four covers from different issues of the same magazine. Use a nail file to open the staples in the centerfold of four of the five identical magazines. Pull out the staples, remove the covers, and substitute the covers from the four issues that are different. Then restaple the four magazines. You now have five identical magazines, each with a different cover.

The volunteer will think the magazines are different issues because the covers are different. When you casually pick up one of the remaining four magazines, you ask the person to choose a number within a range that includes a section where you know there are illustrations on every page. While she is finding the page with the number she chose, you turn to the same page and bring your copy up in front of your face to demonstrate how the subject should hold the magazine so that you can't see the illustration. As you do so, you glance at the illustration on the page your subject has chosen and then close the magazine. Having seen the illustration on the chosen page, you can easily draw or describe it.

SHOW **10**
Possessed Writing

You will need:
- a friend to serve as a medium
- stick, cane, or broom

As reigning "psychic," tell your audience that you are possessed by a spirit that controls your hands as you use a stick, cane, or broom to write messages in "spirit symbols" that your "medium" can read. To convince them of your powers, you ask your medium to leave the room. The audience is then invited to choose an object in the room.

When your medium returns, you begin writing the spirit symbols. The writing consists of a variety of strange signs you make on the floor or ground using your stick, cane, or broom. When you have finished your possessed writing, your medium announces the object that the audience chose.

THE SECRET

Although the audience will concentrate on the symbols you draw with your stick, your medium knows that the symbols are hocus-pocus designed to draw the audience's attention away from what is said. She concentrates instead on what you say and on the number of times you thump the floor or ground with the end of your "writing" instrument.

Suppose the audience has chosen a blue chair. To communicate that to your medium, you begin by saying something that starts with the letter b, such as, "Be ready!" This tells the medium that the name of the object begins with b. Now the medium waits for the second letter so you might say, "Look carefully!" as you furiously draw symbols on the floor. The medium now knows the second letter of the object's name is an l. The third letter is a vowel—u. To indicate vowels, you use the end of the stick, cane, or broom handle to thump the floor. One thump is an a, two thumps is an e, three an i, four an o, and five a u. Since the third letter of blue is u, you thump the end of the stick five times. Then you thump it twice to indicate an e.

You then start on the second word by saying something like, "Consider this,"
as you draw some more weird symbols. Continue to devise words and thumps to
transfer the next four letters of the word chair. When you have finished, you
might ask the medium if she has understood the spirit symbols. She replies, "I
think so. I believe it is the blue chair."

SHOW **11**
Fingers with Eyes

You will need:
- volunteer from the audience
- several bright, easily seen, colored crayons—red, orange, green, blue, purple, and black
- small table covered by an overhanging cloth
- small white card

Ask a volunteer from your audience to sit opposite you at a small table covered by an overhanging cloth so the audience cannot see what goes on under the table. Ask the volunteer to hold a box of crayons beneath the table. Without looking, the person removes one crayon from the box and holds it so you can touch it with your "color-sensitive" fingers. A few seconds later, after some grimacing, you announce the color of the crayon. The volunteer opposite you then holds the crayon so the audience can identify it and see that it is the color you named. If you wish, the show can be repeated with the same or a different volunteer.

THE SECRET

As you read in Chapter 1, the easy way to see with your fingers is to peek! You can
use that method to convince your friends or an audience that you can read with
your fingertips. Or, as in this show, you can demonstrate that your fingers can
"see" colors.

To reveal the color-sensitive nature of your fingers you will need several
crayons that produce bright, easily seen colors. Red, orange, green, blue, purple,
and black are probably the best colored crayons to use.

73

When you use both hands to feel the crayon, your hand away from the audience holds a tiny piece of a white card that you brush against the tip of the crayon that you hold firmly with your other hand. While continuing to feel the crayon with the hand under the table, you glance down at the white card that you hold beside your leg with the other hand.

To repeat the trick, you can simply turn the tiny card over.

SHOW 12
PK Power

You will need:
- overhead projector for large audience; for a small audience, a table will do
- magnetic compass; for a large audience you'll need a compass with glass or plastic on both top *and* bottom, such as an orienteering compass
- screen (if overhead projector is used)

People who claim to have psychokinetic powers often demonstrate it by making a compass needle move without touching it. You can demonstrate your PK power in a similar way.

If you are demonstrating your PK power to a large audience, you'll need a compass with glass or plastic on both top *and* bottom. An orienteering compass works well. Place the compass on an overhead projector and shine its image onto a screen so everyone can see it. With a small audience, you can place the compass on one side of a small table. Stand some distance from the compass as you describe psychokinesis. Then explain that you are going to use your PK power to move a compass needle without touching it. As you get close to the compass, begin moving your hands and grimacing to suggest that PK requires intense mental energy. After the compass needle moves, back away and pretend to be out of breath.

If someone suggests that you are carrying a magnet, let them look at your open hands, take off your coat, and roll up your sleeves.

THE SECRET

Before the show, tape a strong magnet to your body in a place where it cannot be seen. (Under the elastic waistband of your underwear is a good place.)

With the magnet taped to your body beneath your clothing, your secret is safe—unless an audience demands a strip search. Moving hands will help to distract the audience as you move the region of your body to which the magnet is taped close to the compass.

Bibliography

Akins, W. R. *Your Psychic Powers and How to Test Them.* New York: Watts, 1980.

Avery, Michael. *Great Mysteries: ESP: Opposing Viewpoints.* San Diego: Greenhaven Press, 1989.

Christopher, Milbourne. *ESP, Seers & Psychics.* New York: Crowell, 1970.

——. *Mediums, Mystics and the Occult.* New York: Crowell, 1975.

Funston, Sylvia. *Scary Science: The Truth Behind Vampires, Witches, UFOs, Ghosts and More.* Toronto, Ontario: Greey de Pencier Books, 1996.

Hansel, C. E. H. *ESP, A Scientific Evaluation.* New York: Scribner, 1966.

Hopkins, Budd. *Intruders: The Incredible Visitations at Copley Woods.* New York: Random House, 1987.

Nickell, Joe, Barry Karr, and Tom Genoni, eds. *The Outer Edges: Classic Investigations of the Paranormal.* Amherst, NY: CSICOP, 1996.

Randi, James. *An Encyclopedia of Claims, Frauds, and Hoaxes of the Occult and Supernatural.* New York: St. Martin's Press, 1995.

——. *Flim-Flam! Psychics, ESP, Unicorns and Other Delusions.* Buffalo: Prometheus Books, 1982.

——. *The Magic World of the Amazing Randi.* Holbrook, MA.: Bob Adams, 1989.

Sagan, Carl. *The Demon-Haunted World.* New York: Random House, 1995.

UFOs: Encounters and Abductions, VHS Documentary (approx. 100 minutes) Produced by Greystone Productions, Inc., for A&E Network, New York: 1996.

See also various issues of the *Skeptical Inquirer,* published by Committee for the Scientific Investigation of Claims of the Paranormal (CSICOP).

Index

Page numbers in *italics* refer to illustrations.